DEC 2015

Amazing Biomes

TROPICAL RAIN FORESTS

BROWN BEAR BOOKS

Published by Brown Bear Books Ltd

4877 N. Circulo Bujia
Tucson, AZ 85718
USA

and

First Floor
9-17 St. Albans Place
London N1 0NX

© 2015 Brown Bear Books Ltd

ISBN: 978-1-78121-246-2

Library of Congress Cataloging-in-Publication Data
available upon request

Author: Leon Gray
Designer: Karen Perry
Picture Researcher: Clare Newman
Editor: Tim Harris
Children's Publisher: Anne O'Daly
Design Manager: Keith Davis
Editorial Director: Lindsey Lowe

Manufactured in the United States of America

CPSIA compliance information: Batch# AG/5567

Contents

INTRODUCTION

Tropical rain forests grow in warm countries near the **equator**. These dark, rainy **biomes** are home to an amazing variety of animals and plants.

White-lined monkey frogs live on trees in the rain forests of South America.

The places where animals or plants live and grow are called biomes. Some animals and plants live in deserts, grasslands, or oceans. And some have **adapted** to survive in tropical rain forests. Warm, wet rain forests are found in many countries of the world, but they only grow close to the equator between the Tropic of Cancer and the Tropic of Capricorn. These two imaginary lines circle our planet north and south of the equator in an area known as the tropics.

Read on to find out what tropical rain forests are like—and how plants, animals, and people live in them.

WET WORLD

Heavy downpours flow into rivers and streams that flow through tropical rain forests. This water supports the many animals and plants that live there.

5

RAIN FORESTS OF

Rain forests are found in most tropical areas of the world. The largest rain forests are in South America, central Africa, and Southeast Asia.

Dense rain forests cover the tiny Hawaiian island of Oahu in the Pacific Ocean.

The Arenal Volcano looms large above the Monteverde cloud forest of Costa Rica, Central America.

NORTH AMERICA

EUROPE

TROPIC OF CANCER

EQUATOR

SOUTH AMERICA

TROPIC OF CAPRICORN

The Cononaco River snakes through the Amazon rain forest in Ecuador.

ANTARCTI

THE WORLD

RAIN FORESTS

A rain forest in Thailand in Southeast Asia.

ASIA

AFRICA

AUSTRALIA

A photographer on a trip through the rain forests of the Congo River basin, in central Africa.

CLIMATE

Rain forests help to create the rain that gives them their name by playing their part in the **water cycle**. The water cycle is a key reason we have life on Earth.

WATER

In a single year, enough rain falls on the Amazon rain forest to fill 2 billion Olympic-size swimming pools.

Tropical rain forests are warm because they grow close to the equator, where the sun's heat is at its strongest. The heat of the tropical sunshine evaporates the water on Earth's surface quickly, making the air very **humid**. Imagine sitting in a hot bathtub. The steam that fills your bathroom is the water that has evaporated. In the rain forest, the steam is the mist and clouds that form as humid air rises above the forest **canopy**. As it rises, the mist cools and gathers together in water droplets. These fall as rain.

Tropical Storms

Since rain forests are so warm and the air is so humid, thunderstorms are common. Huge clouds build up above the rain forest canopy as more and more water evaporates into the air. As the warm air rises, it cools. The water vapor turns into a liquid, and rain pours down onto the forest below.

Tropical Seasons

The rain forests that grow closest to the equator do not have summers and winters. The climate remains the same all year. At night, the air cools and the temperature of the rain forest falls. During the day, the temperature rises again. As you move farther away from the equator, rain forests have rainy seasons and dry seasons. These seasons happen because of the way Earth tilts as it spins around the sun. The part that tilts toward the sun is warmer, and more rain falls (rainy season). The part that tilts away from the sun is cooler, and less rain falls (dry season).

BIO FACT

Tropical rain forests can soak up heavy rainfall, which prevents flooding. In Bangladesh, where people have cut down many of the trees, there are huge floods every few years.

Tropical Island

Tiny patches of rain forest often thrive on islands in the tropics, such as this one in the Maldives in the Indian Ocean. There are no summers or winters here. The warm sea makes the air humid, creating frequent rainfall that encourages plants to grow.

Some rain forest plants, called **epiphytes**, grow on trees and collect the rainwater that drips down the branches.

PLANTS

Tropical rain forests are home to an enormous variety of plant life, from tall trees that poke above the canopy to tiny shrubs that grow on the forest floor.

The plants in a rain forest grow in a series of layers. The forest floor at the very bottom is covered with moss and other simple plants but mainly with rotting leaves and dead flowers. It is damp and dark because the tree canopy blocks out the sunlight.

The layer above the forest floor is called the understory. It is a dense tangle of shrubs, young trees, and vines. These plants grow in the shade of taller trees, which make up the rain forest canopy. Many types of ephiphytes grow on trees, from the understory to the canopy.

The very tallest trees actually poking through the canopy form the **emergent layer**, which is very sunny during the day because it is above the canopy.

WOW!

● Rain forests are home to some of the tallest trees in the world.

● The Kapok tree grows in the Amazon rain forest, in South America. It can reach up to 220 feet (70 meters) tall. It's trunk measures more than 13 feet (4 meters) across.

BIG ROOTS

The trees in the emergent layer have wide "buttress" roots that spread across the forest floor to support the weight of the tree.

Animal Attraction

Rain forest plants are usually very colorful. The bright flowers are not just for decoration; they help to attract animals such as insects and birds. The flowers produce a sugary liquid called **nectar** and dustlike particles called **pollen**. Birds and insects that are attracted to the colorful flowers are rewarded with a drink of nectar. As they drink, pollen sticks to the bodies of these animals. When the birds and insects visit other flowers, the pollen rubs off on the plant. This process is called **pollination**. It means that the plants can produce fruit and seeds, which are then spread out in the forest and grow into new plants.

Rafflesia Plant

This plant has the largest flower of all plants. It is found only in the rain forests on the islands of Sumatra and Borneo, in Southeast Asia. The giant red-and-white flower is more than 3 feet (1 meter) wide and stinks of rotting flesh! The smell attracts insects, which move pollen from male to female flowers.

FROG FOOD

Beetles and flies live inside the flowers of Heliconia plants, which grow in some rain forests. Tree frogs are attracted to these plants, since they eat insects that live there.

Red-eyed tree frog.

Many rain forest birds, such as the little spiderhunter, feed on the nectar of flowering plants. Spiderhunters also eat spiders.

Tree frogs crawl over flowers in search of beetles and flies.

Insects hide inside the flowers.

ANIMALS

The variety of animal life in the tropical rain forests is astounding—there are more **species** than in almost any other biome on Earth. Scientists are still finding new species.

GORILLAS

Mountain gorillas live in some tropical rain forests in Africa. Young gorillas stay in their family group until they are at least eight years old.

In a South American rain forest, a tree frog waits on a twig until a moth flies past. The frog will catch the moth with its sticky tongue.

Every type of animal can survive in the warm, wet rain forest climate, from insects and birds to reptiles and mammals. Scientists estimate that more than 50 percent of the world's animal species live in the rain forest. Each animal has adapted to its own way of life. It eats specific food, lives in a specific part of the biome, and uses its own set of skills to stay alive.

Rain forests are home to colorful birds, such as these macaws.

Fruit-Eaters

Many different animals survive on the abundant supply of fruit in the rain forest. Since there is no summer or winter in the rain forests near the equator, this fruit food is available all year round. Flowering plants produce fruit to help disperse their seeds. When animals such as bats, birds, and monkeys eat fruit, the seeds in the fruit are either dropped or pass out of the animals' bodies in their poo. The seeds can then grow into new plants where they land—usually far away from the original plant. The animals therefore help the plants to spread through the rain forest.

BIO FACT
Some fruit bats live in rain forests. They fly around the forest in search of small fruit that grows on trees. The bats suck the juice out of the fruit.

Ape Relations

The bonobo is an ape that lives in the dense rain forests of the Congo in Africa. Apes are a group of mammals that includes gorillas, chimpanzees, and humans. Like other apes, bonobos live in groups, and they are very clever animals. Bonobos feed mainly on the plentiful supply of fruit found in the rain forest, but sometimes they hunt other animals for meat.

Rain Forest Predators

The dense vegetation in rain forests is a perfect hiding place for **predators** such as birds of **prey**, reptiles, and big cats. Owls and eagles swoop between the trees feeding on small animals, and crocodiles lurk in rivers and streams to snap up animals that stop for a drink. Snakes and tigers lie in wait to ambush passing prey, such as deer and other smaller mammals.

Nile crocodiles live in rivers that flow through rain forests in Africa. They hunt monkeys, deer, fish, and snakes.

Aerial Attack

The harpy eagle is one of the deadliest predators of the Central American rain forests. These large birds of prey have enormous, sharp, hooked claws (called talons) on their feet, which measure up to 5 inches (13 centimeters) long. They use their talons to pluck sloths, lizards, and other animals from the treetops.

The Brazilian wandering spider uses its deadly venom to kill prey, such as frogs and mice.

BIO FACT
Tigers are top predators that live in the rain forests of South and Southeast Asia.

PEOPLE

From traditional **hunter-gatherers** to the farmers of today, people have been living in harmony with the rain forests for thousands of years. But many others have been exploiting the forests for their rich resources.

MUSIC MEN

People from the village of Kamayura in the Amazon rain forest in Brazil still practice many of their traditions.

Rain forests have been home to people since the very beginning of the human species. The rich variety of plant and animal life has provided people with food, shelter, and medicine.

In remote parts of rain forests, a few people still continue to live a traditional way of life. They hunt wild animals, such as birds, deer, and monkeys, and collect fruit, mushrooms, and nuts from the forest. These hunter-gatherers usually live in small groups. Instead of living in houses, some of them build temporary huts for shelter as they move around the forest. This way of life is dying out, however, as other people clear the forests for farming, raising livestock, and building permanent homes.

In Southeast Asia, people cut the bark of rubber trees to get a white liquid called latex. They make rubber from this.

This traditional longhouse in Borneo is made from the wood of rain forest trees.

Modern Life

Today, most people who live in tropical forest regions have turned to **agriculture** to survive. They have cleared large areas of rain forest to grow crops and raise livestock to feed their families. Rain forests have also been cleared to provide valuable resources, such as coffee, rubber, tea, and spices, which the local people harvest and sell. Cities have been built along the rivers that run through prime rain forest biomes. People have built dams across these rivers, harnessing the heavy tropical rains to generate **hydroelectricity**. Unfortunately, the dams also flood the rain forest, killing the animals and plants that live there.

In the City

Manaus is the capital city of the Brazilian state of Amazonas. It is built on the banks of the Negro River in the heart of the Amazon rain forest. More than 1.9 million people live in this isolated city.

BIO FACT

Many rain forest plants contain amazing lifesaving medicines. Quinine is used to treat malaria. Quinine comes from the bark of the cinchona tree, which grows in the Amazon.

Vast areas of trees in the Amazon rain forest have been felled for agriculture, such as cattle farming.

THE FUTURE

Rain forests around the world are in danger. If these fragile biomes continue to be cleared to satisfy the economic needs of agriculture and industry, many plants and animals will be lost forever.

The future of rain forests is uncertain. A few hundred years ago, these areas of outstanding natural beauty were relatively unspoiled. Today, farmers and loggers have changed the landscape forever. Rain forests are disappearing at an alarming rate. Some people think they could disappear in less than 100 years if this **deforestation** continues. The effects will be devastating. Earth's climate will become warmer, and many rain forest animals and plants may become **extinct**.

Orange Ape

The orangutan is one of the most endangered animals on Earth. A close relative of humans, this orange ape lives in rain forests on the islands of Borneo and Sumatra in Southeast Asia.

Logging is big business and one of the biggest threats facing rain forests around the world.

PALM OIL
Farmers growing palm trees for oil in Malaysia have faced criticism for destroying the country's rain forests and driving many animals to extinction.

QUIZ

Try this quiz to test your knowledge of rain forest biomes. The answers are on page 31.

1 White-lined monkey frogs live in the rain forests of which continent?

2 What is the name of the sugary liquid this bird is drinking?

3 On which islands do the giant red flowers of the Rafflesia plant grow?

What is the name of this city in the heart of the Amazon rain forest?

Fact File

- Most tropical rain forests grow in countries near the equator.

- The climate in rain forests is warm and rainy.

- Rain forests are home to an amazing variety of life.

- Scientists think that rain forests will disappear in 100 years if deforestation continues at its current rate.

Winners and Losers

↑ Farming, logging, and mining provide people in developing countries with jobs and money to feed their families.

⬇ Tigers will become extinct if deforestation continues. One hundred years ago, there were 100,000 tigers in the world's rain forests. Today, there are fewer than 3,200 in the wild.

5 This bird of prey lives in the rain forests of Central America. What is it called?

GLOSSARY

adapted: When a plant or animal has changed to help it cope better in its surroundings.

agriculture: The practice of growing plant crops and raising animals for food, clothing, and other products.

biomes: The places where plants or animals usually live and grow.

canopy: The dense layer of trees and other vegetation that forms the top of a rain forest.

deforestation: The process of clearing trees for agriculture, timber, and/or other human industries.

emergent layer: The tallest layer of trees above the rain forest canopy.

epiphytes: Plants that grow on other plants without stealing the other plants' water or nutrients.

equator: An imaginary line that passes around Earth's widest point.

evaporates: To turn from water to gas when heated.

extinct: When a plant or animal has died out.

forest floor: The bottom layer of the rain forest.

humid: When the air contains a high level of water vapor.

hunter-gatherers: People who collect fruit, berries, and nuts and hunt wild animals for food.

hydroelectricity: The electricity generated from the water that flows through dams.

nectar: The sugary liquid found inside the flowers of some plants.

pollen: Tiny dustlike particles made by the male parts of a flower.

pollination: When an animal transfers pollen from one plant to another.

predators: Animals that hunt other animals, called prey, for food.

prey: Animals that are hunted by other animals, called predators.

species: A group of animals that look alike. Members of the same species can mate and produce young together.

venom: A poison that some animals make in their bodies to attack prey.

water cycle: The journey that water takes as it moves between land, the air, and the oceans.

FURTHER RESOURCES

Books

Newland, Sonya. *Saving Wildlife: Rain Forest Animals.* Mankato, MN: Riverstream Publishing, 2013.

Seymour, Simon. *Tropical Rainforest.* Washington, DC: Smithsonian, 2010.

Tagliaferro, Linda. *Explore the Tropical Rain Forest.* North Mankato, MN: Capstone Press, 2006.

Wojahn, Rebecca Hogue. *A Rain Forest Food Chain: A Who-Eats-What Adventure in South America.* Minneapolis: Lerner, 2009.

Web Sites

Mongabay: Tropical Rainforests
kids.mongabay.com
Check out this great site led by Mongy the bay frog, with awesome photos and videos of rain forest peoples and creatures, plus info about why we should save the rain forests.

National Geographic: 15 Cool Facts about Rain Forests
http://ngkids.co.uk/did-you-know/15_cool_things_about_rainforests
Discover cool facts about rain forests across the globe, from the idiot fruit to black howler monkeys!

Smithsonian: Rainforests
www.stri.si.edu/sites/rainforest/
Read all about how rain forest plants, trees, and animals interact to create a fragile balance in this amazing biome.

World Wide Fund: Amazon
www.worldwildlife.org/places/amazon
View amazing photos and videos of animals and plants that live in the vast Amazon region, home to one in ten known species of plants and animals on Earth. Find out what people are doing to protect this important land and how you can help.

Answers to the Quiz: **1** South America. **2** Nectar. **3** Borneo and Sumatra. **4** Manaus (in Brazil). **5** Harpy eagle.

INDEX